BAPTISM:
The Often Misunderstood Commandment

COMPILED BY L. B. BRAMBLE
& CHUCK WYETH

Additional copies can be ordered in bulk from the publisher.

Published in the United States of America by:

Cobb Publishing
704 E. Main St.
Charleston, AR 72933
www.CobbPublishing.com
CobbPublishing@gmail.com
479-747-8372

ISBN: 9781686885921

Foreword

Baptism: The Often Misunderstood Commandment is intentionally brief and so simple that a child could understand its excellent content. L. B. Bramble and Chuck Wycth provide the truth about baptism as presented in the New Testament. The principles presented by these brethren are backed up solidly by Scripture.

Leaders of congregations will want to order the brief volume in bulk to be distributed far and wide. Anyone who wishes to teach the truth about New Testament baptism will thankfully accept this little volume as a beautiful evangelistic tool.

Unless one has unsound presuppositions, it is difficult to believe anyone could read this book and still be confused about the subject and necessity of baptism.

The chapters are brief. Even a slow reader can complete the entire volume in less than an hour.

For veteran Christians, Bramble and Wyeth's brief study will strengthen your faith and hopefully encourage you to reignite the flame of evangelism that may have turned to embers. The motivation of the authors is to teach the truth, not about making a name for themselves.

I recommend *Baptism: The Often Misunderstood Commandment* without reservation. It should become a classic for those who love the truth and seek to honor God's command.

Dr. Ted Burleson,
Preacher, Hamilton (Aabama) Church of Christ

Associate Professor, Turner School of Theology, Amridge University, Montgomery, AL

Introduction

This book is deliberately small and easy to read. It is written so anyone who reads it can understand. It is short, sweet, and to the point.

Baptism is, as the title suggests, often misunderstood. But as you look to the Word of God, without the doctrines of men clouding the issue, you'll find the topic is actually quite clear.

Throughout this book, we will constantly point you to Scripture as the authority—because ultimately, it isn't what we say, or what anyone else says that matters. It's what God says that matters.

We pray that you will be blessed and edified by this work.

The Authors

Contents

A Typical Story about Children

One day a parent walked into their child's room and saw paper lying on the floor. They promptly told the child to pick the paper up, as it was a hazard and they could slip and fall because of it. The parent further told the child that for doing this simple task, they would take them out at the end of the day for a special treat.

The child, when they thought their parent was not watching, kicked the paper under the nearest piece of furniture where they presumed it would be out of sight. What they didn't know was that their parent saw them do it.

Question: Does the child deserve the treat that was promised?

We'll come back to this story later on...

Chapter 1
The Great Commission

Jesus, as one of the final statements to His apostles, gave what is often called —The Great Commission. In doing so, He made baptism an essential element of making disciples.

> *And Jesus came up and spoke to them, saying, "All authority has been given to Me in heaven and on earth. Go therefore and make disciples of all the nations, baptizing them in the name of the Father and of the Son and of the Holy Spirit, teaching them to observe all that I commanded you; and low, I am with you always, even to the end of the age." (Matthew 28:18-20, NASB)*

The question, though, is this: *How did such a clear and simple statement turn into a muddy theological battle?* It doesn't have to be confusing, if one simply goes by what the Bible says on the topic.

Chapter 2
But What Constitutes Baptism?

The word *baptism* comes from the Greek word *baptizo*, a derivative of *bapto, to dip, immerse, submerge for a religious purpose.*[1] The word for pouring and the word for sprinkling are never translated as baptism, because those words have different meanings.

Baptism is also a burial.

> ***Colossians 2:12*** *having been **buried with Him in baptism**, in which you were also raised up with Him through faith in the working of God, who raised Him from the dead. (NASB)*

Can you bury anything by sprinkling *(Greek rhantizo)* or pouring *(Greek ekcheo)* on it? NO! They do not fit the Bible's definition! The **one true Baptism** can only be performed by immersing a person in water. In fact, there is no dispute that this was the only practiced form of baptism for hundreds of

---

[1] Definitions of **baptizo, bapto**, also including **baptisma** and **baptismos**, come from "The New Strong's Expanded Exhaustive Concordance of the Bible." James Strong, LL.D., S.T.D.

years after Christ, until men, using human wisdom, brought in pouring and sprinkling. *(Infant christenings will be discussed later.)*

Note:

> ***Ephesians 4:4-6*** *There is one body and one Spirit, just as also you were called in one hope of your calling; one Lord, one faith, **one baptism**, one God and Father of all who is above all and through all and in all. (NKJV)*

If we are to understand the meaning, purpose, and practice of baptism, we must look to the word of God for our answers. Why? Because the word of God is our only reliable source for all things in religion.

When Jesus went into the desert for 40 days, His first temptation was to turn stones into bread so He could eat (Matthew 4:4). But He answered and said,

> *"**It is written**, Man shall not live by bread alone, but **by every word that proceeds from the mouth of God.**" (NKJV)*

And look at 2 Timothy 3:16:

All Scripture is given by inspiration of God, and **is profitable** for doctrine, for reproof, for correction, for instruction in righteousness, that the man of God may be **complete**, thoroughly equipped for every good work. (NKJV)

Thus, this subject must be taken seriously by us all.

Note: Paul clearly states there is only one baptism, which rules out the idea of sprinkling and pouring in its place, as these would be other forms, violating that scripture.

Chapter 3
Old Testament Preparation
for New Testament Baptism

God actually prepared His people for the acceptance of baptism in several different ways—over a thousand years before Jesus gave that Great Commission!

Travel back in time to the Exodus,[2] when the children of Israel were delivered from their Egyptian bondage.

> ***1 Corinthians 10:1-2*** *Moreover, brethren, I do not want you to be unaware that all our fathers were under the cloud, all passed through the sea, all were **baptized** into Moses in the cloud and in the sea, all ate the same spiritual food, and all drank of that spiritual Rock that followed them, and that Rock was Christ. (NKJV)*

Note: In the Red Sea crossing, God parted the waters, and the children of Israel passed

---

[2] The Exodus took place around 1440 BC (though some say as late as 1250 BC). This shows God's planning and forethought in preparing His people's minds to accept baptism.

through the sea, now saved from the Egyptians—just like we are now saved from our sins through baptism.

Also note: as they pass through, the water—towering high on both sides, with the cloud above them—symbolized the baptism (immersion in water) that was to come. (Moses in the Old Testament, who they were baptized into, is used like a type of Christ, who came later at His appointed time.)

The children of Israel had been prepared for the coming of the Messiah. One of those ways was in ritual washing.

Note: *Mikvah, Ritual Baths.* The word —mikvah‖ (also, mikveh, mikva, miqve) means collection and refers to a collection of water that was used for ritual immersion in Judaism. The Jews would purify themselves before several activities or after certain events that made them unclean. Conversion to Judaism requires submersion into a mikvah. The area around the Temple Mount, especially to the south, is filled with mikvah. A mikvah had to have a source of running water, such as a spring, or a stream. A mikvah had to be large enough to allow an average-sized person to immerse his whole body. Stairs would be used to descend into and ascend from the mikvah. Often there was a wall separating the clean side from the unclean side.[3]

This is seen most clearly when it comes to those who would act as priests to our living God:

> ***Exodus 40:12-15*** *"Present Aaron and his sons at the entrance of the tabernacle, and wash them with water. Dress Aaron with sacred garments and anointing him, consecrating him to serve me as a priest. Then present his sons and dress them in their tunics. Anoint them as you did their father, so they may also serve me as priests. With their anointing, Aaron's descendants are set apart for the priesthood forever, from generation to generation." (NLT)*

Note: Aaron and his sons, who were to be anointed into the priesthood, needed to be clean to minister unto God. Thus, the command, "wash them with water."

---

[3] Information on Mikvah, Ritual Baths was attained from generationword.com & wikipedia.org.

*Exodus 30:17-21 Then the Lord spoke to Moses, saying, "You shall also make a laver (washbasin) of bronze, with its base also of bronze, for washing. You shall put it between the tabernacle of meeting and the altar. And you shall put water in it, for Aaron and his sons shall wash their hands and their feet in water from it. When they go into the tabernacle of meeting, or when they come near the altar to minister, to burn an offering made by fire to the Lord, shall wash with water, **lest they die**; So they shall wash their hands and their feet, **lest they die**. And it shall be a statute forever to them, to him and his descendants throughout their generations." (NKJV)*

Note: "that they may not die" is emphasized twice—that's a warning.

Note: Aaron and his sons not only had to be anointed (i.e. washed) and consecrated to do their job, they still had to wash their hands and their feet every time they were to enter the tent of meeting to perform their service, or they would die.

Now the question may arise in some of you—"What is the point that he is trying to make?" or "What does this have to do with baptism?"

Hebrews 8:1-7 Now the main point in what has been said is this: we have such a high priest (i.e. Jesus), who has taken his seat at the right hand of the throne of the Majesty in the heavens, a minister in the sanctuary and in the true tabernacle, which the Lord pitched, not man. For every high priest is appointed to offer both gifts and sacrifices; hence it is necessary that this high priest also have something to offer. Now if He were on Earth, He would not be a priest at all, since there are those who offer the gift according to the law; who served a copy and shadow of the heavenly things, just as Moses was warned by God when he was about to erect the tabernacle; for, "See," He says, "that you make all things according to the pattern which was shown you on the mount." But now He has obtained a more excellent ministry, by as much as He (i.e. Jesus) is also the mediator of a better covenant, which has been enacted on better promises. For if that first covenant had been faultless, there would have been no occasion sought for a second. (NASB)

Hebrews 9:11-28 *But when Christ appeared as a high priest of the good things to come, He entered through the greater and more perfect tabernacle, not made with hands that is to say, not of this creation; and not through the blood of goats and calves, but through His own blood, He entered the holy place once for all, having obtained eternal redemption. For if the blood of goats and bulls and the ashes of a heifer sprinkling those who have been defiled sanctify for the cleansing of the flesh, how much more will the blood of Christ, who through the eternal spirit offered Himself without blemish to God, cleanse your conscience from dead works to serve the living God?*

For this reason, He is the mediator of a new covenant, so that, since a death has taken place for the redemption of the transgressions that were committed under the first covenant, those who have been called may receive the promise of the internal inheritance for where a covenant is, there must of necessity be the death of the one who made it. For a covenant is valid only when men are dead, for it is never in force while the one who made it lives. Therefore, even the first covenant was not inaugurated without blood. For when every commandment has been spoken by Moses to all the people according to the law, he took the blood of the calves and the goats with water and scarlet wool and hyssop, and sprinkled both the book itself and all the people, saying "Thus is the blood of the covenant which God commanded you." And in the same way he sprinkled both the tabernacle and all the vessels of the ministry with the blood. And according to the law, one may also say, all things are cleansed with blood, and without shedding of blood there is no forgiveness.

Therefore, it was necessary for the copies of the things in the heavens to be cleansed with those but the heavenly things themselves with better sacrifices than these. For Christ did not enter a holy place made with hands, a mere copy of the true one, but into heaven itself, now to appear in the presence of God for us; nor was it that He should offer Himself often, as the high priest enters the holy place year by year with blood not his own. Otherwise, He would have needed to suffer often since the foundation of the world; but now once at the consummation of the ages He has been manifested to put away sin by the sacrifice of Himself. And inasmuch as it is appointed for men to die once and after this comes judgment, so Christ also having been offered once to bear the sins of many, will appear a second time for salvation without reference to sin to those who eagerly await Him. (NASB)

Note: The tabernacle and priesthood were a copy and shadow of the heavenly things, requiring repetitive sacrifices. But Jesus' sacrifice was once for all time.

> **Hebrews 9:28** *so Christ also, having been offer once to bear the sins of many, shall appear a second time for salvation without reference to sin, to those who eagerly await him.*

Now put this with 1 Peter 2:4-5.

> *Coming to Him as to a living stone, rejected indeed by men, but chosen by God and precious, you also, as living stones are being built up as a spiritual house **a holy priesthood**, to offer up spiritual sacrifices acceptable to God through Jesus Christ. (NKJV)*

Notice the parallel to this in Exodus 19:6.

> *And you shall be to me **a kingdom of priests** and **a holy nation.** These are the words which I shall speak to the children of Israel. (NKJV);*

or

> *and you will be **My kingdom of priests, My holy nation**. (NLT)*

Note: In the Old Testament, the children of Israel were in a sense God's priests to the world starting with an imperfect high priest such as Aaron. Under the New Testament, Christians are God's priests to the world with the only begotten Son of God as the high priest. The washing in order to consecrate Aaron and his sons to the priesthood was pointing forward to the "washing of regeneration" (i.e., baptism/immersion) that makes us Christians and thus part of the priesthood of God.

> *Galatians 3:26-27 So in Christ Jesus you are all children of God through faith, for all of you who were baptized into Christ have clothed yourself with Christ. (NASB)*

> *And all who have been **united with Christ in baptism** have put on Christ, like putting on new clothes. (NIV)*

Note: The garment we have been given is Christ Himself through baptism, our act of faith through submission. Is this not like a parallel to Aaron and his sons receiving holy (or sacred) garments in Exodus 40:13?

Note also: A person is baptized *into* Christ. According to the wording of the Greek, we are "baptized into His possession." (NASB) or "united with Christ in baptism" (NLT). Therefore, it is our submission to baptism (as He commanded) that truly adds us to His body. Nowhere else does God show any other way to become part of Christ's body.

Again, in 1 Peter 2:9:

> *But you are a chosen race, **a royal priesthood**, a holy nation, a people for God's own possession, that you may proclaim the excellence of Him who has called you out of the darkness into His marvelous light.*

Think about what took place in the Parable of the Marriage Feast, Matthew 22:11-13.

> *"But when the king came in to look over the dinner guests, he saw there a man not dressed in wedding clothes, and he said to him, 'Friend, how did you come in here without wedding clothes?' And he was speechless. Then the king said to the servants, 'Bind him hand and foot, and cast him into the outer darkness; in*

that place, there shall be weeping and gnashing of teeth.'"

Note: The wedding guest was not dressed in the proper apparel. This suggests strongly that without being baptized into Christ, into His possession, putting on Christ, we would be in the wrong apparel when Christ returns. Therefore we would be rejected.

Chapter 4
The Wisdom of God

1 Corinthians 1:20-25 Where is the wise man? Where is the scribe? Where is the debater of this age? Has not God made foolishness the wisdom of the world? For since in the wisdom of God the world through its wisdom did not come to know God, God was well-pleased through the foolishness of the message preached to save those who believe. For indeed Jews ask for signs, and Greeks search for wisdom; but we preach Christ crucified, to Jews a stumbling block, and to Gentiles foolishness, but to those who are called, both Jews and Greeks, Christ the power of God and wisdom of God. Because the foolishness of God is wiser than men, and the weakness of God is stronger than men. (NKJV)

Let me approach this subject this way:

People are not afraid to bathe in the water. They aren't afraid to go to the beach to swim and play in the water. People dive from high places into the water, even making contests of who can do it best. People put on equipment and dive deep in the ocean for exploration and research.

Yet the idea of baptism causes many to hesitate! **Why?** It certainly isn't because they are afraid of water.

Could it be people think of it as foolishness?

Chapter 5
Prophecy of John the Baptist

Luke 3:3-6 *Then John went from place to place on both sides of the Jordan River,* **preaching that people should be baptized to show that they had repented of their sins and turn to God to be forgiven.** *Isaiah had spoken of John when he said, "He is a voice shouting in the wilderness, prepare the way for the Lord's coming! Clear the road for him! The valleys will be filled, and the mountains and hills made level. The curves will be straightened, and the rough places made smooth. And then all the people will see the salvation sent from God." (NLT)*

Concerning John the Baptist, the Bible states:

Luke 7:24-28 *When the messengers of John had departed, He (i.e. Jesus) began to speak to the multitudes about John, "What did you go out into the wilderness to see? A reed shaken by the wind? But what did you go out to see? A* *man clothed in soft garments? Indeed, those who are gorgeously apparel and live in luxury are in kings' courts! But what did you go out to see? A prophet? Yes, I say to you, and more than a prophet. This is he of whom it is written, [Malachi 7:8] "Behold, I send my messenger before your face, Who will prepare your way before you! For I say to you, among those born of woman there is not a greater prophet than John the Baptist; but he who is least in the kingdom of God is greater than he." (NKJV)*

Matthew 3:6 *and were being **baptized** by him in the Jordan River, confessing their sin. (NKJV);*

"Confessing their sins, they were baptized by him in the Jordan River." (NIV)

"and when they confessed their sins, he baptized them in the Jordan River." (NLT)

Note: John was not a man dressed in a fancy suit like some preachers today at a big gathering. He was not in a fancy building or stadium, but was in the wilderness living off the land. He did not have a fancy baptistery; he baptized *(immersed)* people in a river. The people came to John so that they could hear the message and do that which was right before God.

*Matthew 3:13-17 Then Jesus arrived from Galilee at the Jordan coming to John to be baptized by him. But John tried to prevent Him, saying "I have need to be baptized of You and do You come to me?" But Jesus answering said to him, "Permit it at this time; for in this way it is fitting for us to fulfill all righteousness." Then he permitted Him. After being **baptized (immersed)** Jesus came up immediately from the water and behold, the heavens were opened, and he saw the Spirit of God descending as a dove and lighting on Him, and behold, a voice out of the heavens said, "This is my beloved Son, in whom I am well-pleased." (NASB)*

1 Peter 3:18-22 For Christ also died for sins once for all, the just for the unjust, so that He might bring us to God, having been put to death in the flesh, but *made alive in the spirit; in which also He went and made proclamation to the spirits now in prison, who once were disobedient, when the patience of God kept waiting in the days of Noah during the construction of the ark, in which a few, that is, eight persons were brought safely through the water. Corresponding to that, baptism **(immersion)** now saves you – not the removal of dirt from the flesh, but an appeal to God for a good conscience – through the resurrection of Jesus Christ, who is at the right hand of God, having gone into heaven, after Angels and authorities and powers had been subject to Him. (NASB)*

Note: Baptism is not for *physical* cleansing but a *spiritual* cleansing. It is also an act of righteousness which Jesus fulfilled, being our example. (Remember, Jesus had no sin to wash away.)

Chapter 6
*Baptism Continued through
the New Testament Record.*

__John 4:1-2__ Jesus was making and baptizing more disciples than John (although Jesus Himself was not baptizing, but His disciples were.) (NASB)

After Peter's preaching on the day of Pentecost, the people asked, "Brethren, what shall we do?"

__Acts 2:38-39__ Peter said to them, "Repent, and each of you be baptized in the name of Jesus Christ for the forgiveness of your sins; and you will receive the gift of the Holy Spirit. For the promise is for you and your children and for all who are far off, as many as the Lord our God will call to Himself." (NASB)

__Acts 2:41__ so that, those who had received His word were baptized __[immersed in water]__; and that day there were added about 3,000 souls. (NASB)

__Note__: Repentance therefore is a prerequisite for being baptized (cleansed)! Remember, John the Baptist paved the way for Jesus, and taught baptism for the remission of sins. If you look at Paul's travels, while in Corinth, he ran into some disciples that had only known the baptism of John the Baptist.

> ***Acts 18:4-6*** *Then Paul said, "John indeed baptized with a baptism of repentance, saying to the people that they should believe on Him whom would come after him, that is on Jesus Christ." When they heard this, they were baptized in the name of the Lord Jesus. And when Paul had laid hands on them, the Holy Spirit came upon them… (NKJV)*

One can see by this that repentance is very important, but they still needed to be baptized into the possession of Christ.

Special Note 1: Some people claim that since Jesus forgave the sins of the thief upon the cross, it somehow reduces the importance of baptism (immersion) for the remission of sins.

First, one must understand that the thief lived and died under the Old Testament, the Law of Moses. Baptism was never commanded to be right with God under that law.

Second, one must also understand Jesus was still alive (He had not yet died, been buried, or resurrected—the events which give baptism its meaning) and He was able to forgive in the same manner that you have the right to give your possessions away while you are alive. Once Jesus was crucified, buried, and resurrected, the Law of Christ came into effect, which includes the necessity of baptism for the remission of sins (Mark 16:15-16).

> *Hebrews 9:16-17 For where there is a testament, there must also of necessity be the death of the testator. For a testament is in force after men are dead, since it has no power at all while the testator lives. (NKJV)*

Special Note 2: In the Bible, there is no mention of any infant being christened. We learned earlier that one needed to believe in order to be baptized. Does an infant have that kind of capability of understanding? And how can they repent of sins if they do not even understand the concept of sin? Infants and children are very much like Adam and Eve in the garden prior to partaking of the forbidden fruit. That's why Jesus said in Mark 10:14-15:

"Permit the children to come to Me; do not hinder them; for the kingdom of God belongs to such as these. Truly I say to you, whoever does not receive the kingdom of God like a child shall not enter it at all." (NASB)

Mark 9:36-37 *Then He took a little child and set him in the midst of them. And when He had taken him in His arms, He said to them, "Whoever receives one of these little children in My name receives Me; and whoever receives Me, receives not Me but Him who sent Me." (NKJV)*

Matthew 18:3-6 *and said, "Truly I say to you, unless you are converted and become like little children, you will not enter the kingdom of heaven. Whoever than humbles himself as this child, he is the greatest in the kingdom of heaven. And whoever receives one such child in My name receives Me; but whoever causes one of these little ones who will believe in Me to stumble, it would be better for him to have a heavy millstone hung around his neck, and to be*

28

drowned in the depths of the sea."
(NASB)

Matthew 18:10 *see that you do not despise one of these little ones, for I say to you that their angels in heaven continually see the face of My father who is in heaven. (NASB)*

Jewish people hold their bar mitzvah for children at 13, as they consider that the age of accountability. I personally see children maturing at varying rates. I further understand that God is righteous and will be a just judge. In the end, I can only conclude from the verses stated above that children are safe to a point, but I cannot pinpoint a specific time where they would become accountable for sins.

That said, infant christenings still do not make any sense, and have no scriptural foundation at all. Besides not having the ability to believe, and having no sins to repent of, the mode is all wrong too. It is still just sprinkling and pouring, which has already been proven not to be a true form of baptism (immersion).

I have seen children brought up in the knowledge and understanding of the Lord, and they will seek to be baptized for the remission of their sins when they realize their state in sin.

I would also strongly urge anyone who was sprinkled, poured, or christened as a child to be properly baptized, immersed in water for the remission of their sins, as they certainly are now accountable and have the capability of belief and repentance.

In Acts 9:1-18, Saul was heading toward Damascus to persecute Christians and was confronted by the Lord. Jesus explains to him the error of his way and he became blind and was taken on to Damascus. A man named Ananias came to speak to Saul, who afterwards received his sight. In the 18th verse, Saul got up and was baptized. Paul retells the story of his conversion in Acts 22. Verse 16 relates what he was told by Ananias:

> *"Now why do you delay? Get up and be baptized, and wash away your sins, calling on His name." (NASB)*

In Acts 8, we find the story of the Ethiopian eunuch, who Philip taught on the desert road. The results are seen in verses 36-39.

*As they went along the road they came to some water; and the eunuch said, "Look! Water! What prevents me from being baptized?" and Philip said, **"If you believe with all your heart, you may."** and he answered and said, "I believe that Jesus Christ is the son of God." And he ordered the chariot to stop; and **they both went down into the water, Philip as well as the eunuch,** and he baptized ["bapto," immersed] him. When **they came up out of the water**, the spirit of the Lord snatched Philip away; and the eunuch no longer saw him, but went on his way rejoicing. (NASB)*

Note: Here we can again plainly see that one must believe to be baptized. But as we have no promise of tomorrow, we always see an urgency in being baptized (immersed in water) for the remission of sins. The idea of immersion is further shown by both going down into the water and coming back out. He also rejoiced because his sins had been forgiven!

Romans 6:1-7 What shall we say then? Are we to continue in sin so that grace may increase? May it never be! How shall we who died to sin still live in it? Or do you not know that all of us who have been baptized into Christ Jesus have been baptized into His death? Therefore, we have been buried with Him through baptism into death, so that as Christ was raised from the dead through the glory of the Father, so we too might walk in newness of life. For if we have become united with Him in the likeness of His death, certainly we shall also be in the likeness of His resurrection, knowing this, that our old self was crucified with Him, in order that our body of sin might be done away with, so that we would no longer be slaves to sin; for he who has died is free from sin. (NASB)

Note: Baptism has other symbolic meanings, according to God. When a person is baptized, they go down into the water and are immersed in the water just as a person who has died is buried in the ground. When one comes up out of the water it is in the same likeness that Jesus rose from the dead. This cannot take place by someone pouring a trickle of water on your head or sprinkling a few drops over you. Baptism is an immersion in water—nothing more, and definitely nothing less. How many may be lost in the world today because they do not understand the importance of baptism?

> *1 Corinthians 12:12-13 For even as the body is one and yet has many members, and all the members of the body, though they are many, are one body, so also is Christ. For by one Spirit we were all baptized into one body, whether Jews or Greeks, whether slaves or free, and we were all made to drink of one Spirit. (NASB)*

Note: So, by one Spirit we were all baptized into one body. How can you be part of the one body without being properly baptized?

> *Hebrews 10:19-22 Since therefore, brethren, we have confidence to enter the Holy Place by the blood of Jesus, by a new and living way which He inaugurated for us through the veil, that is, His Flesh, and since we have a high priest*

*over the house of God, let us draw near
with a sincere heart in full assurance of
faith, having our hearts sprinkled clean
from an evil conscience and our bodies
washed with pure water.*

Note: This reference once again goes back
to the idea of the priesthood. Jesus is in
place of Aaron, the High Priest, and we take
the place of his sons. The Old Testament
priesthood was a shadow of Christians in
Christ today. Likewise, our bodies washed
with pure water signifies baptism.

Colossians 2:12 *having been buried
with Him in baptism,* ***in which*** *you were
also raised up with Him* ***through faith***
*in the working of God, who raised Him
from the dead. (NASB)*

Note: This signifies that baptism is also an
act of faith in God.

Chapter 7
Baptism is a Necessity

John 3:1-8 *Now there was a man of the Pharisees named Nicodemus, a ruler of the Jews; this man came to Jesus by night and said unto Him," Rabbi, we know that You have come from God as a teacher; for no one can do these signs that You do unless God is with Him." Jesus answered and said to him, "Truly, truly, I say to you, unless one is born again he cannot see the kingdom of God." Nicodemus said to Him, "How can a man be born when he is old? He cannot enter a second time into his mother's womb and be born can he? Jesus answered, "Truly, truly, I say to you, unless one is born of water and the Spirit he cannot enter into the kingdom of God. That which is born of the flesh is flesh, and that which is born of the Spirit is spirit. You must be born again. The wind blows where it wishes and you hear the sound of it, but do you know where it comes from and where it is go-*

ing; so is everyone who is born of the spirit." (NASB)

Note: Unless one is born of water (i.e. immersed in water for the remission of sins) and the Spirit (its result, Acts 2:38) he cannot enter into the kingdom of God.

Chapter 8
Baptism versus Works

Many today say baptism is a work. They use Scriptures like **Ephesians 2:8**, and assert that baptism is under consideration there.

> *"For by grace you have been saved through faith, and that not of yourselves; it is the gift of God, not of works, lest anyone should boast."*

Therefore, as some consider baptism a work, they wrongfully conclude it is not necessary. So, let us look at the Scriptures to see what they actually say.

The Great Commission, found in **Matthew 28:19**, states,

> *"Go therefore and make disciples of all the nations, baptizing them in the name of the Father and of the Son and of the Holy Spirit."*

Note that it instructs the disciples to do the baptizing. It does not instruct them to teach someone to baptize themselves. If the apostles are doing the baptizing, they are the ones doing the work. The one being baptized is, by faith, submitting to God's will, making themselves available to the one doing the baptizing. In other words, it can't be a work if it is something done *to* you.

Note also **Matthew 3:13-14**

Then Jesus arrived from Galilee at the Jordan coming to John to be baptized by him. But John tried to prevent Him, saying "I have need to be baptized of You and do You come to me?"

Clearly, Jesus came to the Jordan River to be baptized by John the Baptist. Likewise, John the Baptist exclaimed he needed to be baptized by Jesus. Both make it clear that they could not do this to or for themselves. Likewise, we can clearly see that a baptizer, (one who does the baptizing) and the one to be baptized are both needed for a baptism to take place.

Likewise, **John 4:1-2**

"Jesus was making and baptizing more disciples than John (although Jesus Himself was not baptizing, but His disciples were,") (NASB)

Here we see again clearly that the one being baptized needs someone to baptize them. John the Baptist baptized Jesus; in turn Jesus baptized His disciples who in turn baptized others that came to them. Always there is someone there to baptize the repentant person who needs God's forgiveness.

The word "works," found in Ephesians 2:9, comes from the word *"ergon,"*[4] which means *'work,' 'deed,'* or *'business.'*[5] These are words of action which signify the person doing them is putting forth physical effort in order to achieve a purpose.

So, the question is, *is the person being baptized putting forth physical effort in order to achieve a purpose*? We can clearly see that it takes energy to go down into the water and to come back out again, but clearly many people walk into the water and come back out again and are not baptized. Going into the water is merely a preparatory step but it is not baptism. Also exiting the water is after the fact, what is left?

Simply this, at the point of baptism, the one doing the baptizing places their hands on the one to be baptized in a way that will allow them to dip/immerse this person in water

---

[4] Our word *ergonomic* comes from this word.
[5] Young's Analytical Concordance.

and bring him back up again. The baptism is then scripturally completed in the name of the Father, the Son, and the Holy Spirit. The person being baptized expends no energy in the process, as they are only submitting to the one doing the baptizing.

Therefore, baptism is not a work as mentioned in **Ephesians 2:9** as far as the one being baptized is concerned. A more accurate description is that *baptism is a submission, because of faith, to God's will.* Their faith causes them to allow another Christian to dip/immerse them in water, with faith that God will forgive them of their sins (**Matthew 3:6-7**; **Acts 22:16**); that they are baptized into Christ Jesus *(i.e. into Christ's possession)* (**Romans 6:1-7**, **Galatians 3:27**); baptized into His death, burial, and resurrection so that they will see newness of life; and as Christ rose from the dead, so also will they rise from the dead as promised (**Romans 6:1-7**); and will be translated into the kingdom of God (**John 3:1-8; Colossians 1:13**).

Chapter 9
Points

1. Baptism is part of the great commission given to the apostles who handed it down to those who are Christians today. **Matthew 28:18-20**

2. The preparation for the New Testament baptism was started as far back as the exodus of the children of Israel from Egypt. **1 Corinthians 10:1**

3. John the Baptist fulfilled the prophecy to prepare the way for Jesus' ministry (**Mal. 7:8, Luke 7:24-28**), and he baptized people for the remission of their sins. (**Matthew 3:6-7** & **Acts 22:16**)

4. Baptism is an act of righteousness (Matthew 3:13-17), and an act of faith (Colossians 2:12). In the truest sense, *"baptism is a submission, because of our faith, to God's will."*

5. Jesus was baptized despite having no sin. **(Matthew 3:13-17)**. The disciples also were baptized and then baptized those that they taught. **(John 4:1-2)**. It is a simple matter of history that people are still being baptized

(immersed) for remission of their sins by the true church of Christ.

6. The disciples taught about baptism and its importance through their ministry. (**John 4:1-2**, **Acts 2:38-41; 8:36-38; 9:18**)

7. Those baptized are baptized into Christ Jesus *(i.e. into Christ's possession)* (**Romans 6:1-7**, **Galatians 3:27**). There is no other Scripture showing any other way to get into Christ's possession.

8. When baptized into his death, we are buried with him through baptism into death, so that as Christ was raised from the dead, so we too can walk in newness of life. (**Romans 6:1-7**)

9. We are baptized into one body. (**I Corinthians 12:12-13**)

10. Those baptized into Christ have put on Christ as we put on a garment. (**Galatians 3:27**)

11. There is only one baptism. (**Ephesians 4:4-6**)

12. A person cannot see or enter The Kingdom of God without being born again, in other words baptized. (**John 3:1-8**)

13. *The people needed to be clean before they could be in the presence of God. Those in the priesthood even more so* **(Exodus 19:10-11; 19:14; 40:12-15; 30:17-21)**. This was a shadow or copy of heavenly things **(Hebrews 8:1-7; 9:24-25)**. In the same manner that Christ died once, being the perfect sacrifice for sin, we need once to be baptized *(dipped or immersed)* in a more perfect covenant, unlike the priests under the Mosaic Law which had to wash every time they were to perform their duties as priests. *There is a distinct parallel between the Old Testament priest and the new testament Christian – called a royal priesthood* **(1 Peter 2:4-5, 9)**. *We need to be clean* (i.e. baptized) *in order for our sacrifices to God to be acceptable to God!*

14. Again, if we look back at the original language we can plainly see that the word baptism comes from the word *baptizo* which correctly translated would mean to be **dipped**, **submerged**, or **immersed** *in water*. So, to be baptized correctly according to the Scriptures, you must go down into the water and be dipped or immersed in the name of the Lord Jesus. And if you now go back over all the previous Scriptures and use the term

"dipped" or "immersed" in the place of the word "baptism," it has a much clearer meaning. For in the same likeness as Jesus went into the ground after death and was raised up again three days later, we are buried in water as our fleshly desires are dead and we are raised up in newness of a spiritual life in Christ Jesus.

Note: For 251 years, baptism was clearly done through immersion. At that time, a man named Novatian was believed to be near death due to a life-threatening disease. Believing in the necessity of immersion for salvation, but having put baptism off and now unable to leave his bed, he didn't know what to do. Some men substituted the profuse pouring of water, in order to simulate immersion, all about him while he lay in bed. There was no such authority for such an action, and the events set off a controversy throughout the whole church body. Clearly, the wisdom of men was used instead of the command given by God.

Chapter 10
A Warning

We read several instructions that God handed down to the people through Moses in **Leviticus 6:12-13**.

> *The fire on the altar shall be kept burning on it. It shall not go out, but the priest shall burn wood on it every morning; and he shall layout the burnt offering on it, and offer up in smoke the fat portion of the peace offering on it. (NASB)*

Leviticus 10:1-2 shows the consequences of not loving God enough to do things exactly as he instructs.

> *Now Nadab and Abihu, the sons of Aaron, took their respective fire pans, and after putting fire in them, placed incense on it and offered **strange fire** before the Lord, **which He had not commanded them**. And fire came out from the presence of the Lord and consumed them, **and they died before the Lord**. (NASB)*

Men, using human wisdom not from God, have replaced baptism (immersion) in many instances with sprinkling and pouring—and even infant christenings which were never done in the Bible. God's words are what we are to live by, not man's **(Matthew 4:4).** To count on the unfounded teachings of men will be as disastrous for us as the offering of strange fire was to Nadab and Abihu.

If we love God, we must keep His commandments and be clean to stand before Him. Baptism must be done in the manner prescribed by God if it is to be pleasing to God.

Baptism (root "bapto," immersion) must be done in the manner prescribed by God if we want to have our sins forgiven.

Also, after becoming a Christian through following the Bible pattern, we need to continue faithful until death to inherit eternal life (Revelation 2:10).

Also, **Ephesians 5:25-27** says:

> *Husbands, love your wives, just as Christ also loved the church and gave Himself up for her, so that He might sanctify her, **having cleansed her by the washing of water** with the word (NKJV).*

The King James Version says "by the word." The New Living Translation says "by the cleansing of God's word." The New American Standard says it this way:

> *That he might present to Himself the church in all her glory, having no spot or wrinkle or any such thing; but that she would be holy and blameless. (NASB)*

Now back to where we began, the great commission Jesus gave to His disciples and all those who would follow Him. **Matthew 28:18-20**:

> *And Jesus came and spoke to them, saying, "All authority has been given to Me in heaven and on earth. Go therefore and make disciples of all the nations, **baptizing** ("bapto," immersing) them in the name of the Father and of the Son and of the Holy Spirit, teaching them to observe all things that I have commanded you; and low, I am with you always, even to the end of the age" (NKJV).*

But note this other warning from **Matthew 7:21-23**:

*"Not everyone who says to Me, 'Lord, Lord,' will enter the kingdom of heaven, but he who does the will of My Father who is in heaven will enter. Many will say to Me on that day, "Lord, Lord, did we not prophesy in Your name, and in Your name cast out demons, and in Your name, perform many miracles?' And then I will declare to them, 'I never knew you; **depart from me, you who practice lawlessness**'" (NASB).*

Or "ye that work iniquity" (KJV); "you who break God's laws" (NLT).

Have the people you listen to concerning God and His teaching been true to this great commission given by Jesus

And more importantly, have you been properly baptized (immersed) for the remission of your sins (Acts 2:38-39; 22:16; 16:33) and into Christ, that is, into his Possession (Romans 6:1-7, Galatians 3:26-27)?

Conclusion to
"A Typical Story about Children"

Hopefully you still remember the story in the front of this book, about a parent asking a child to do a simple task: pick up a piece of paper. Instead, the child assumed that what the parent really wanted was just to not see the piece of paper. Therefore, this child decided there was an easier way—a *better* way—to follow the parent's instruction and receive the promised treat at the end of the day.

What the child really did was exchange what they were actually told for something simpler and easier for them, and justified the disobedience to the clear command with their own childlike reasoning.

Question: Does the child deserve the special treat they were promised?

Question: How does this story compare to your decision about being baptized?

My Faith Statement

by Earl Chuck Wyeth

[Note: I was requested to write out the core, foundational items of my faith as part of entrance into a Christian college. I was encouraged to include it here as well.]

I believe God is the creator of all things. I believe God created everything that exists in six days, and on the seventh day He rested, as stated in Genesis. I believe He spoke through prophets of old and through His Son Jesus Christ.

I believe Jesus is the Son of the living God, and that He, the Father, and the Holy Spirit are one. I believe the only way to have salvation is through the blood of Christ and the only way we have that salvation is through the death, burial, and resurrection of Jesus. We receive our salvation through the forgiveness of sins, which happens only when we hear, believe, confess, repent, and are immersed in the waters of baptism for the forgiveness of sins, into the possession of Christ and receive His Holy Spirit (Acts 2:38).

I believe baptism now saves us (1 Peter 3:21). I believe we need to follow the example of Jesus' life in order to enter heaven. I believe nothing I do as a Christian is going to save me: that only comes by grace through the blood of Christ.

I believe I cannot save anyone, and that only God adds us to His church according to Acts 2:47.

I believe the Bible is the word of God and is true and that to know Him, we must first study the words which He inspired in the Scriptures. I believe we are commanded not only be baptized, but I take Matthew 28:18–20 as a command—we must spread the gospel and baptize others. I also believe Ephesians 4:1-6 is something that we must abide by and know is true.

Lastly, I know I will one day be with Him in heaven (1 John 5:13). We have that assurance. I also believe that without faith it is impossible to please God, for he who comes to God must believe that He is and that He is a rewarder of those who diligently seek Him (Hebrews 11:6). And the way I know these things is by looking at the facts directly in the context of the Bible.

Made in the USA
Columbia, SC
09 June 2021

39569020R00033